BEST OF IRISH
POTATO
RECIPES

DELICI〇

Irish

BASED ON TRADITIONAL IRISH COOKING

PRAISE FOR THE *BEST OF IRISH* COOKBOOKS:

'This series is fabulous and highly recommended. The books
are packed full of information ... A handy and very
neat addition to any kitchen shelf'
Books Ireland

'Exciting Irish cookbook series.
Easy to follow, zippy and well presented'
Carla Blake, Irish Examiner

'An easy-to-carry gift to bring home as a souvenir of a visit'
RTÉ Guide

'Sound recipes with an Irish flavour ...
And they are quite straightforward'
Georgina Campbell, Irish Independent

BIDDY WHITE LENNON is a founder member and currently Chairwoman of the Irish Food Writers Guild. Her previous cookbooks include *The Leaving Home Cookbook, Irish Traditional Cooking* and *The Eating at Home Cookbook*. She has written and presented a ten-part television series on healthy eating for the Irish Department of Health.

Biddy writes regularly for *Food and Wine Magazine*, has a cookery column in the *Irish Farmers' Journal* and a column in *Woman's Way* magazine. She gives cookery demonstrations all over Ireland and is a freelance contributor to many publications and a regular broadcaster on television and radio on subjects as varied as health, social welfare, fashion, interiors and travel.

As an actress, she is perhaps best known in Ireland for her portrayal of Maggie in the hugely popular RTÉ television series, *The Riordans*, a role she played for fifteen years. She continued to act in the series when it moved to radio and also co-wrote many episodes with her husband, later writing for the TV series *Glenroe*.

Best of Irish Potato

RECIPES

BIDDY WHITE LENNON

THE O'BRIEN PRESS

DUBLIN

First published 2002 by The O'Brien Press Ltd,
20 Victoria Road, Dublin 6, Ireland.
Tel: +353 1 4923333; Fax: +353 1 4922777
E-mail: books@obrien.ie
Website: www.obrien.ie
Reprinted 2003.

ISBN: 0-86278-759-9

British Library Cataloguing-in-Publication Data
White Lennon, Biddy
Best of Irish potato recipes
1.Cookery (Potatoes) II.Cookery, Irish
I.Title II.O'Hara, Anne III.Irish potato recipes
641.6'52'09415

2 3 4 5 6 7
03 04 05 06 07 08

Editing, layout, typesetting, design: The O'Brien Press Ltd
Author photograph: Peter Orford
Illustrations: Anne O'Hara
Cover photography: Walter Pfeiffer
Printing: Cox & Wyman Ltd

Are you from Ireland?
I am, are you?
Do you eat spuds?
I do, do you?
How do you eat them?
Skins and all.
Do they choke ye?
Yerrah, not at all!

Contents

Introduction

No one really knows how the potato reached Ireland. According to legend, Sir Walter Raleigh (he of the Virgin Queen, a puddle of water and his cloak) introduced it to his estate at Youghal, County Cork, at the end of the sixteenth century. There is absolutely no proof of this. Even if he did, he would have got the tubers from England and not from South America, as legend has it.

The diet of the native Irish was built around two main staples: the so-called *bán bhianna* (white foods) – milk, butter, whey and curds – during the summer months when they could graze their livestock; and oats and some other grains during the winter. Should the autumn grain crop fail in any way the winter months would have been hard. The potato offered a second option. By the 1640s it was a field crop in County Wicklow and there is evidence to suggest that by the 1660s and 1670s it had already afforded relief in areas where the grain harvest had failed.

Potatoes thrive on rain and Ireland gets plenty of that; it was only a matter of time before people realised just how well the potato cropped here. Our climate favoured the potato in other ways, too. The Gulf Stream keeps the south and west of the country mild in winter despite the northern latitude, and we get relatively little snow or frost. Our springs, summers and autumns are usually cool and moderate, giving the potato a long, late, growing season. The prevailing southwesterly winds tended to fend off various diseases which periodically attacked potato crops on the European mainland.

Even so, the potato took a good while to establish itself in the Irish diet. A famine (1728–1729), which killed thousands of people, was caused by the failure of the oat crop. Clearly such shortages still could not be made up by the potato crop alone. The oat crop failed again in 1740 and the following winter was very severe. Potatoes that had been stored for the winter in pits above ground were destroyed by freezing. The death toll in the resulting famine possibly reached 400,000.

What was needed was a variety of potato that stored well in damp Irish conditions. Such a cultivar, the Irish Apple, appeared during the 1770s and was the key to the potato becoming the main staple food of the Irish poor – by 1780 a commentator could observe that 'the common Irish' subsisted on potatoes and milk the year round.

The Irish peasantry lacked ploughs and those few who had even primitive versions more often than not lacked the horse or bullock to pull them. However, they all had the spade (or loy) and goodly numbers of men knew how to use it. Over centuries they had developed the 'lazy bed' system of ridge planting – wide, banked seed-drills separated by narrow trenches. This was well suited to the cultivation and harvesting of potato tubers as it provided necessary drainage and ten men could prepare an acre a day to accept tubers, which would then yield between six and eight tonnes per acre.

The remains of 'lazy bed' potato ridges can still be seen on the hillsides in mountainous regions of Ireland (particularly in the West). Despite its name, constructing a lazy bed is no task for a lazy man. First you must haul seaweed (or whatever manure is to be found) to build enough soil on stony ground. It must then be piled up into a ridge – necessary to allow excess water to drain off – and the tubers planted on top. The potatoes, if you were lucky enough to get a crop that wasn't blighted, had then to be carried back down the mountain.

When the household conditions in which the bulk of the people lived are added into this social equation (conditions which made anything but the simplest cooking a major chore), then the potato could seem to have been designed specifically to suit Ireland and the Irish – 'Sure, even a child could cook potatoes!' It has been argued that, in Ireland, potatoes were the first convenience food.

Between 1780 and 1841 the Irish population doubled from about four million to eight million. That this growth in population coincided with the growing dominance of the potato in the Irish diet is too striking to be unconnected. It has been argued that the abundant, prolific and therefore cheap potato encouraged early marriage and that early marriage increased the birth rate. But these arguments rage to this day. What is nowhere in dispute is the calamity that visited the Irish in the middle of the nineteenth century. It was directly proportional in its horror to the Irish reliance on the potato as the main, often the only, food.

Lest anyone suspect that any laziness of the Irish contributed to this disaster, just remember the words of that cantankerous Englishman

William Cobbett, in other circumstances no lover of Ireland, when he pleaded for the repeal of the Act of Union of Great Britain and Ireland:

'Can it be a lazy people [the Irish] who feed the world?* Can it be a good government under whose laws and regulations this laborious people are living on roots, weeds or half stinking mussels? ... No! Every reasonable man in this world will exclaim no it cannot be a good government.'

The Great Famine of 1845 to 1849 and its heart-rending consequences need no further retelling here. What is clear is the fact that, once the immediate horrors of the Famine were past, the potato did not disappear from Irish tables. Nor has it done so since.

The relationship between an Irishman and the plain, unadulterated, boiled floury 'spud' is unique. My own son, who left for university in England at eighteen and still lives and works there ten years later, comes home regularly and always says, 'Jeyes, Ma! It's wonderful to taste real potatoes again!'

Now, down the years, I've been much diverted by calculations made about just what amount of potatoes the nineteenth-century Irish peasant consumed each day. No one disputes that it was a lot – the man of the house probably averaged eight to ten pounds a day! Dieticians ask whether such a diet could possibly be healthy. But, if the Irish family had a cow or access to dairy products, then these contained the calcium and vitamin A the potato lacks.

And never be tempted to doubt the amounts. I remember an elderly (admittedly large, very hardworking) actor who sat down each weekday to three pounds of spuds at lunchtime and would happily eat the same again each evening for dinner.

I also remember being in a good restaurant in the far West of Ireland one Saturday evening only two years ago. In came four fine, big, mountain farmers in town for a night out – pints of stout and a feed. To accompany their main courses a waitress brought them a very (very) large basket of delicious potatoes boiled in their skins. The four men waited patiently, not touching their food. Sensing that something was wrong, the headwaiter came over and asked,

'Is everything OK?'

'We're waitin' till *all* of us have our spuds,' came the (to them)

perfectly reasonable reply.

The Irish have many fond names for the potato: praties and pirtas (from the Irish *prátaí*), poppies, pop-pops, puddies, taties, tatties, balls of flour, murphies and spuds. You will also hear about 'laughing' potatoes. These are potatoes boiled in their skins. When the skins split during cooking, as they often do, it can look as if the spuds are smiling. In England in the nineteenth century, 'Spud Murphy' became the generic nickname for an Irish labourer (Murphy being the commonest Irish surname and potatoes his staple food). More recently, when the confident Celtic Tiger Irish seemed to have taken over the worlds of British business and entertainment, they became generically known in the press as 'the Murphia'.

'Spud' is one of those words that tantalise etymologically. Many words of Irish origin are blatantly labelled 'of unknown origin' in Oxford's great dictionaries. Originally the name for a short blade, as far as I can work it out, 'spud' was later applied to a three-tined fork that would probably have been widely used to lift potatoes from the drill by thousands of Irish 'tattie-hokers' who went annually to Scotland to harvest the potato crop. Interestingly enough, and perhaps to clinch my argument, the procedure used when commencing to drill an oil-well is also known as 'spudding'. Just the Irish being creative with the English language again?

[*Irish beef, both preserved and on the hoof, continued to be exported throughout the Famine.]

Potatoes Then and Now

Sometime between 1780 and 1845 – the year of the first great potato blight – a variety of potato called Lumper became the mainstay of Irish potato plantings (along with the less popular Cups, which were said to 'stay too long in the stomach'). The Lumper was more prolific than the better-keeping Irish Apple but proved disastrously unable to withstand the attack of blight that then visited the country. It is often forgotten now that the potato blight visited many other European countries in those years, but because their economies and diets were not so bound up with the potato crop they survived – battered, starved, desperate –

but spared the overwhelming catastrophe of the Irish Famine.

The disaster of the Famine forced great Victorian fruit and vegetable experts, like Paterson, Nicholl, Sutton and Clark, to embark upon a sustained programme to breed potato cultivars more suited to conditions in Britain and Ireland. By the early 1900s rather more than half a million acres of potatoes were being grown annually in Ireland.

Today, the Irish potato crop divides into three crop seasons: First Earlies (like Homeguard), Second Earlies (like Queens) and Maincrop (older varieties, like Kerrs Pink, Golden Wonder, Record, King Edward, and newer varieties, like Rooster, Pentland Dell, Maris Piper and Cara).

The Irish love of the 'floury' potato has led them to value this quality in a potato above all others. But the rise of the huge supermarket chains who demand regular-shaped, even-sized, washed pre-packs has forced growers to meet this demand. This has led to ritual moans from the Irish potato-loving public that potatoes aren't what they used to be: 'they've no flavour' and 'you can't beat a bit of good honest dirt on a spud!'

Whatever the reason, in recent years the potato has ceded ground somewhat, in the diet of the younger generation certainly, to pasta, to rice and even to pocket breads (Indian naans, Turkish pittas and flour tortillas) as the staple of choice.

But there's still no real problem, as long as you're prepared to put in a bit of effort, in finding the genuine article – thousands of farmers and gardeners still grow their own potatoes, using farmyard manure and even seaweed to 'give them a bit of flavour'. And let's face it, there's just no substitute for an honest-to-God spud taken straight out of the ground just before cooking.

Choosing your Potato

There are two main potato types: the waxy and the floury. Floury potatoes are best for baking, mashing and chipping; waxy for sautéeing, gratinées and for salads. For potatoes that are to be boiled and eaten plain, or with a knob of butter, you may choose either type, but the 'soapy' taste of the waxy varieties is completely alien to the Irish palate. Many imported varieties from Cyprus, Egypt, Italy and France, which are increasingly available in supermarkets towards the end of the season (before the First Early Irish-grown new potatoes arrive), fall into the waxy category or somewhere between and are not really that suitable for traditional Irish dishes – some work, some don't.

As a rough guide (you will have to find your own local potato varieties), I find that Kerr's Pink, Golden Wonder, King Edward, Cara, Rooster and Cultra (to a lesser extent) are the most suitable maincrop varieties for boiling or steaming. For baking there is nothing to approach large Golden Wonders. For puréeing, Golden Wonder still beats everything; but Kerr's Pink, Pentland Dell and Maris Piper can all work. For deep frying (of which I do very little and never with early potatoes), I find Wilja the best early variety, and for main crop I use Desirée, Cara, Pentland Dell and King Edward. For roasting I use Golden Wonder by choice, but Desirée, Rooster, Maris Piper, King Edward and Cara all work fine. For salads, I tend to use only tiny potatoes straight out of the ground – I know where they were grown and the variety doesn't really matter – however, small Rooster, Desirée and Cultra all work and (inevitably) very small Golden Wonder impart a richness of flavour.

So, what's the spud that must be preserved at all costs? Repeat after me … 'Golden Wonder!'

BOILED POTATOES

In Ireland potatoes are boiled 'in their skins' or, as they say in Ulster, 'in their jackets'. After cooking they are peeled at the table and any 'eyes' easily removed. In olden days people who lived by the sea boiled their potatoes in sea water because it is said that, this way, no matter how floury the potato the skin will not split or crack so none of the mineral content is lost.

Boiled potatoes should be served at once. If they are to be mashed or peeled, always do this while the potatoes are hot.

TO BOIL OLD POTATOES

Wash thoroughly but do not peel. Discard any with black or green pieces and remove any sprouts. Cover with cold water. Add enough salt to make the water quite salty. Cover. Bring to the boil and boil steadily until tender. Drain at once and dry by placing a clean tea-towel on top and leaving them on a very low heat for a few minutes. Do not replace the lid.

TO BOIL NEW POTATOES

Wash the potatoes. Do not peel them. Have ready a pot of boiling, salted water, just enough to cover the potatoes. Put potatoes into the boiling water and bring back to the boil quickly; boil steadily until tender. Drain, then place a tea-towel on top of the potatoes and leave them to dry over a very low heat for just a few minutes.

Old Ways: In 1791 an eminent Dublin physician prescribed potatoes for women who were childless.

STEAMED POTATOES

The Irish love of floury potatoes makes keeping the skins intact a constant problem. Steaming potatoes takes a little longer, but it's a small price to pay for relatively intact skins.

Place boiling water in the bottom of the pot and washed potatoes in the steamer; steam until tender. Dry in the usual manner. Steamed potatoes will hold for longer without spoiling. Simply pull the steamer off the heat but do not drain or dry until you are ready to serve.

Traditionally potatoes cooked in their skins (boiled or steamed) are served with a small side plate placed on the left-hand side of the dinner plate. The potato is served from a potato ring or serving dish onto this plate and peeled using a knife and fork. The skins are left on the plate and the potato is lifted onto the dinner plate.

potatoes in colander

ROAST POTATOES

The perfect roast potato starts when you choose the right variety of potato. Guess what? A floury one works best! New potatoes do not roast well, nor does a soapy variety of potato. Size hardly matters — you'll be cutting them into pieces about the size of a golf ball anyway. Never peel potatoes until just before you cook them — potatoes for roasting do not improve sitting in water, and out of it they discolour. Some people swear by parboiling for a few minutes before roasting. I'm not one of them. You will get far crisper results if you roast the potatoes raw and they will absorb less fat.

SERVES 4

Ingredients:

700 g/1 ½ lbs floury potatoes, peeled

2 tablesp sunflower oil, groundnut oil, olive oil, or goose fat

Method:

Cut the potatoes into even-sized pieces and dry them well. Put oil in a roasting tin large enough to hold one layer without crowding. Heat the oil/fat at 210°C/420°F/Gas 6-7. Tip the potatoes into the hot fat (avert your face, it may splatter). Turn the potatoes over to coat with fat on all sides. Place near the top of the oven and cook, turning every so often to ensure that they are golden-brown and crisp on all sides, for about 1 hour. Season and serve as soon as they are done — roast potatoes do not keep well, even in an oven at low heat.

fANNEÒ spuòs

This is a version of Swedish Hasselback potatoes and makes a very decorative, fan-shaped potato for those occasions when you are cooking a dinner to impress. In Ireland, an early season potato from Italy or Cyprus, or a similar yellow-fleshed variety that is not too waxy and is oblong in shape (rather than round), is the best choice.

SERVES 4

Ingredients:

8 oblong, medium-sized potatoes

2 cloves garlic, peeled and crushed

sprigs of fresh rosemary and thyme, chopped, **or** fresh bay leaves, torn into pieces

2 tablesp olive oil

2 tablesp salted butter, melted

freshly ground black pepper and sea salt

Method:

Cut away a small slice from one long side of each potato so that it will sit steady. Now make regular slices widthways, almost to the base of each potato, taking care not to cut all the way through. Use a sharp knife and make the cuts about 4 mm apart. Roll the cut potatoes in the olive oil and butter, season and sprinkle with herbs (if using bay leaves, insert pieces of the leaves into the cuts in each potato). Bake at 200°C/400°F/Gas 6 for about 1 hour, or until they are tender, brown and crisp and the cuts have opened out into a fan shape.

potato chips

You might think the perfect chip is easy to achieve – it most emphatically is not!
I know people who like soggy chips – I've no doubt they're well able to find a way of
cooking them without my help. The following method is the best way I know to
achieve a pile of crisp, golden chips, which you may, if you wish, call French fries.
First choose the right potato – you need a big, floury variety. You will also need a lot
of fresh, high-quality fat. Lard (beef fat) does actually make the best chips, but
sunflower oil is an acceptable, more heart-friendly substitute.

SERVES 4

Ingredients:

4-6 large, floury potatoes

a deep-fat fryer,
three-quarters full of fat/oil

salt

a little patience!

Note:

There are people who like a snack called a 'chip butty'. This involves buttering slices of fresh white pan bread, filling them with freshly cooked (still hot), salted and vinegared chips, then eating the butty at once. It's not exactly a heart-healthy dish, but I'm told by those who love them that if the chips are good, butties are 'to die for'!

Method:

Peel the potatoes. Cut them into long slices about 1 cm/½ inch thick . Then cut each slice lengthways several times (you are aiming for a chip about the size of an average woman's index finger). Drop the chips into a bowl of cold water. Heat the fat until the thermostatic control registers 150°C/300°F. Drain the chips and dry thoroughly with a clean tea-towel. Place in the frying basket and lower them into the fat. Cook for 5 minutes until they are soft but still pale in colour. Lift the basket and drain. Turn the thermostat up to 185°C/365°F, and when the control registers that heat lower the basket into the fat and fry again for 3-4 minutes, shaking the basket a few times to make sure the chips brown evenly. Lift out when golden brown and crisp and tip onto copious amounts of kitchen paper. Sprinkle with salt and serve in a hot serving-dish, or directly on to the plates.

Game Chips

These are not chips in the Irish sense of the word, although they are in the American sense. It is the traditional name in English for wafer-thin slices of deep-fried potatoes. Commercial potato crisps (which most nearly resemble game chips) are made from a variety called Record, a potato still widely available in Ireland. They do indeed make an excellent game chip. A contemporary spin on this dish is to mix the potato slices with very thin slices of root vegetables: celeriac, parsnip, or carrot.

SERVES 4

Ingredients:

350 g/12 oz floury potatoes, peeled

deep-fat fryer, three-quarters full of oil

sea salt, ground

Method:

Slice the potatoes into wafer-thin slices using a mandolin (or a food processor disc). Heat oil in a deep-fat fryer to 190°C/375°F. Fry the potato slices in small batches for 2-3 minutes per batch, or until they turn a rich golden colour and the oil stops sizzling. Drain well, then spread on kitchen paper on a platter. Turn the thermostat up to 200°C/400°F and fry again for 1 minute. Drain well on absorbent kitchen paper and sprinkle with finely crushed sea salt.

CRISP SPICED WEDGES

Wedges are not a traditional Irish recipe. They started life as a commercial dish, mainly on pub menus, but they are now undeniably popular with children of all ages.

SERVES 4

Ingredients:

700 g/1½ lbs yellow-fleshed or floury potatoes, peeled

1-2 tablesp olive oil

1 tablesp paprika

1 heaped teasp tropical (or black) peppercorns, freshly ground

Method:

Cut the potatoes into quarters or eighths, depending on size. Mix the spices, salt and oil and rub this evenly on all sides of the potatoes. Spread out on a flat non-stick baking sheet, taking care not to crowd the potatoes together. Bake at 210°C/420°F/Gas 7 for about 45 minutes, or until crisp and brown on all sides. You will need to turn the potatoes at least once during the cooking time. Serve very hot.

Variations:

It's fun to experiment with different combinations of spices – chosen to complement the rest of the meal. Ground cumin works well with Indian dishes, or add some chopped mint (when serving) to give a North African flavour.

Herbed wedges are popular, the most common combination being rosemary and garlic. In place of the paprika use 1 tablespoon of fresh rosemary, chopped finely, 1-2 cloves of garlic, peeled, crushed and chopped, then proceed as above.

Fresh sage also works (not dried – you will end up with musty, attic-flavoured potatoes!)

BAKED POTATOES

Choose as large and unblemished a floury potato as you can find. Wash it, dry it and prick it at least once with the point of a knife or with a fork. Place it on a baking sheet or directly on the oven rack and bake at 220°C/425°F/Gas 7 for 1–1¼ hours, until completely soft inside when tested with a skewer, and really crisp on the outside. Serve in a basket so that no steam collects during the meal to spoil the crisp skin. Cut in half lengthways and season with salt and black pepper. Serve with butter, sour cream, or crème fraîche, with chopped chives, or chopped mint or parsley.

BAKING POTATOES
IN A MICROWAVE

This is actually a contradiction in terms as, of course, the skin will never crisp. What you can do if you are in a hurry is half-cook the potato in the microwave. The time this takes is directly related to the number of potatoes you are cooking together (4 large ones need about 15 minutes to get to the half-cooked stage – time enough for the oven to get up to heat). Transfer to an oven and bake at 245°C/475°F/Gas 9 for 20-30 minutes.

BAKED POTATO SKINS

Cut large, raw, baking potatoes into wedges and bake at 200°C/400°F/Gas 6 for about 40 minutes, or until tender. Scoop out most of the flesh and use for another purpose. Brush the skins with oil and roast at the same temperature for about 10 minutes (or deep-fry) until crisp. Drain on absorbent kitchen paper and serve with a dip: mayonnaise flavoured with garlic, guacamole, sour cream, or salsa.

SOUFFLÉ BAKED POTATOES

SERVES 4

Ingredients:

4 large floury potatoes

45 g/1½ oz/3 level tablesp butter, melted

100 ml/3½ fl oz/(generous) ½ cup double cream

2 eggs

Method:

Wash, dry and stab each potato with a fork. Bake at 200°C/400°F/Gas 6 until tender (1-1½ hours). Using a sharp knife take a slice lengthways about one quarter way down the potato. With a spoon, scoop all the flesh from the potatoes into a bowl. Separate the yolks from the whites of the eggs. Mix the potato flesh with the melted butter, the cream and the egg yolks and season to taste. Whip the egg whites with a pinch of salt until stiff. Fold gently but thoroughly into the potato mixture. Pile carefully back into the potato skins. Bake at the same temperature for about 15 minutes, or until the soufflés are well risen and tinged with gold.

Serve immediately or (like all soufflés) they will collapse.

STUFFED BAKED POTATOES

The possibilities of stuffing ingredients for this old favourite are virtually endless. Really, the only rule is to choose combinations that have a natural affinity with potatoes.

Method:

Having baked the potatoes in the usual way, scoop out the hot potato flesh from its skin, mix it with the other chopped ingredients, season to taste, spoon it back into the skins and reheat in the oven until hot through.

For the filling: cheese of pretty well any variety is good, as is chopped, crisply cooked bacon, cooked ham, smoked trout, cooked or smoked mackerel, haddock, cod, or salmon, cooked mushrooms, cooked spinach, sweet peppers, tomatoes and herbs.

POTATOES BAKED IN OIL, LEMON AND GARLIC

A dish inspired by Mediterranean cooking that needs potatoes typical of that region – firm, yellow-fleshed ones. In Irish shops, Cyprus or Italian potatoes are probably the best choice.

SERVES 4–6

Ingredients:

900 g/2 lbs yellow-fleshed potatoes, peeled

60 ml/2 fl oz/¼ cup olive oil

125 ml/4 fl oz/½ cup fresh lemon juice

90 ml/3 fl oz/³⁄₈ cup water

2-3 cloves of garlic, peeled, crushed and finely chopped

1 tablesp fresh oregano or marjoram, finely chopped, or 2 teasp dried

Method:

Peel the potatoes. How you cut them depends on size; if small, leave whole; if medium-size, cut in half lengthways; very large ones can be cut into quarters or even eighths. Mix all the ingredients except the potatoes together. Pour this dressing into a large, flat dish (a lasagne dish works well) and season with salt and freshly ground black pepper. Put in the potatoes, turning them so that they are well coated in dressing. Bake uncovered at 230°C/450°F/Gas 8 for about an hour. Check to see they do not dry out too much, adding a little extra warm water if needed in the early stages. Give them an occasional stir so that they cook and brown evenly. They are done when tender, golden-brown and crisp.

oil lemon & garlic…

SINFUL SPUDS (POTATOES BAKED WITH CREAM AND GARLIC)

There is an eighteenth-century saying that the food of the poor was 'small scabby potatoes, and milk having its brains beat out with a stick'. In cabins all over Ireland buttermilk – a by-product of making butter, which was sold to pay rent – was the most frequent 'savour' (flavouring) for boiled potatoes. The inhabitants of the Big House could afford to use cream. This gorgeous dish, inspired by French cuisine (but often spoiled by the addition of cheese), remains one of the most enduringly popular ways of cooking potatoes in Irish homes and in restaurants.

SERVES 4–6

Ingredients:

900 g/2 lbs waxy, yellow-fleshed potatoes, peeled and thinly sliced

2-3 cloves garlic, peeled, crushed and chopped

200 ml/7 fl oz/¾ cup cream

3 tablesp chopped parsley or chives* (optional)

a knob of butter

*Herbs add flavour but take from the pale-gold appearance of this classic dish.

Method 1:

Grease a wide, flat dish with a little butter. Layer the potatoes, garlic and herbs, seasoning each layer as you go. Do not build up to more than six layers of potatoes. Pour the cream over the potatoes (it should reach to just below the top layer). Bake at 160°C/325°F/Gas 3 until the potatoes are tender and the top golden. Depending on how thick the layers of potatoes are this will take 1½-1¾ hours. To get the correct texture it's important to press the potatoes down several times during the first hour of cooking. Rest in a warm place for 8-10 minutes before serving.

Method 2:

A quicker, but not as good, way of cooking this dish is to cover it with foil and bake at 200°C/400°F/Gas 6 for about 1 hour. Remove the foil about 15 minutes before the end of the cooking time to allow the top to brown.

Variation:

For a less sinful dish, substitute milk for cream (using sufficient milk to come just level with the top layer of potatoes. It takes slightly longer to cook whichever method you use.

Variation:

Substitute chicken or vegetable stock for the milk, and sprinkle about two tablespoons of grated Irish Gabriel cheese, or Parmesan, or vintage cheddar cheese over the top layer about halfway through the cooking time.

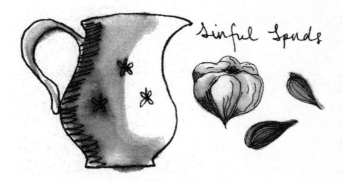

Sinful Spuds

POTATO AND MUSHROOM BAKE

This makes a good dinner-party dish or a vegetarian main course. Its origins, like many another Irish dish, are French. Real goose fat turns this from interesting to sublime. The type of mushroom used depends on availability. Mixed wild mushrooms work well, so too do mixed, cultivated 'wild' mushrooms from a supermarket. And, although the finished dish will not be as interesting or complex in flavour, it's a good way to cook common cultivated mushrooms with potatoes.

SERVES 4

Ingredients:

450 g/1 lb waxy potatoes, peeled

200 g/7 oz wild mushrooms

90 g/3 oz/(generous) 1 cup goose fat, or oil and butter mixed

2 large cloves of garlic, peeled, crushed and chopped

2-3 shallots, or one small onion, peeled and finely chopped

2 tablesp parsley, chopped

Method:

Chop the mushrooms into fairly large pieces. In a heavy frying-pan melt 2 tablespoons of the fat. Add the mushrooms, season with salt and pepper and fry briskly, stirring, until the mushrooms are tender and any moisture from them has been cooked off. Add the garlic and the shallots or onion and cook for a few moments before stirring in the parsley.

Slice the potatoes very thinly using a mandolin or food processor slicer. If slicing by hand aim for about 3 mm/⅛ inch thick.

Melt two tablespoons of fat in an oven-proof pan or skillet about 20 cm/8 inches wide. Remove from heat. Arrange half the potato slices in the pan in overlapping circles. Season with a little salt and pepper. Spread the mushroom mixture on top. Arrange the remaining potatoes on top of the mushrooms. Finish with the remaining fat. Cover with foil and place a weight on top of that. Cook on the hob for 6-7 minutes until the bottom is beginning to brown, then place in an oven at 190°C/375°F/Gas 5 for about 20 minutes. Remove from oven, remove weight and foil cover. Place a dinner plate on top, then invert the pan, transferring its contents to the plate. Slide them back into the pan, pale side down. Cook for another 5 minutes. Serve hot, cut into triangles.

Cheese Potato Croquettes

SERVES 4

Ingredients:

700 g/1 ½ lbs floury potatoes

2 egg yolks

4 tablesp freshly grated
Gabriel cheese, or Parmesan

2 scallions, finely chopped

1 tablesp butter

3 tablesp parsley, finely
chopped

For the coating:

2 whole eggs, lightly beaten

fine white breadcrumbs

plain white flour

Method:

Steam the potatoes with their skins on, dry, then peel. While hot put through a potato ricer, a mouli, or mash thoroughly. Add egg yolks, cheese, chopped scallions, butter, salt and black pepper (to taste). Shape into small walnut-sized balls, or cork shapes. Place some flour and breadcrumbs on separate plates and set up a production line. Roll each ball or cork in flour first, then dip in the beaten egg, then coat with breadcrumbs. Leave in a cool place to set for at least 30 minutes. Deep-fry at about 190°C/375°F in oil until golden brown and crisp. For an extra-crisp coating fry for 1 minute, drain them well, then fry again for 2-3 minutes.

Variation:

Plain potato croquettes can be made by omitting the cheese and scallions; use about 60 g/2 oz butter and 1 egg (or the equivalent amount of milk).

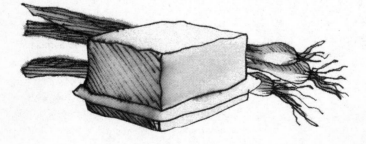

IRISh POTATO SALAD

This is one of the very few potato dishes that Irish people concede needs a firm, waxy potato for success.

SERVES 4

Ingredients:

450 g/1 lb waxy new potatoes

4 scallions, finely chopped

2 tablesp fresh mint, finely chopped

2 tablesp olive oil

125 ml/4 fl oz/½ cup mayonnaise

60 ml/2 fl oz/¼ cup milk

Method:

Whisk the milk and mayonnaise together. Scrub the new potatoes – if they are truly new and fresh, their skins will be removed by a brisk scrubbing. Old, waxy potatoes should be peeled when cooked. Steam the potatoes until just tender, taking care not to overcook them. Drain, dry and, while still hot, cut into cubes of a size that pleases you. Sprinkle the olive oil over them while still hot and season with salt and freshly ground black (or white) pepper. Cool to room temperature and then gently stir the mayonnaise mixture and the scallions through the potatoes. Finally sprinkle with chopped fresh mint.

Variations:

Add 3-4 streaky bacon rashers (grilled until crisp then crumbled) with herbs. Try different herbs singly or in combinations (chosen to complement the rest of the meal) – chives, wild garlic, parsley, marjoram, dill leaves, fennel leaves.

Substitute 150 ml/5 fl oz/½ cup sour cream or crème fraîche for the mayonnaise and omit the milk.

Instead of mayonnaise, dress potatoes with vinaigrette and a tablespoon of capers, drained, dried and chopped.

POTATO STUFFING

In County Kerry this stuffing is known as 'pandy'. No goose is complete without a generous amount of potato stuffing to soak up some of the gorgeous goose fat (it's pretty effective with duck as well). The herb you choose is up to you. If you are eating this stuffing with pork, goose or duck, fresh sage is traditional; thyme, winter savoury and parsley are other possibilities, either singly or mixed. Traditionally, stuffing was placed in the body cavity of the bird, however, to avoid any danger of cross-contamination, food safety experts say it is wiser to stuff only the crop (neck) and to ensure that the stuffing is completely cold before being placed in the bird.

SERVES 6

Ingredients:

900 g/2 lbs floury potatoes, cooked, dried and mashed

450 g/1 lb onion, peeled and chopped

2 large apples, peeled, cored and chopped (optional)

225 g/½ lb lean sausage meat (optional)

1 tablesp butter, or goose fat, or duck fat

Method:

Put the potatoes in a large mixing bowl. Melt the butter or goose fat in a pan and in it sweat the chopped onion and apple. Pan-fry the sausage meat, breaking it up with a fork until browned and cooked through. Add the onion, apple, cooked sausage meat (if using) and herbs to the potatoes. Season to taste with salt (very little if you are using sausage meat) and freshly ground black pepper. Cool stuffing thoroughly. Stuffing is best made the day before roasting the goose.

To Stuff a Goose/Duck:

Immediately before cooking, lightly pack the neck cavity of the bird and sew up the opening. Always weigh the bird when stuffed, to calculate the cooking time. Any remaining stuffing can be cooked in a greased dish in the oven for about 40 minutes.

champ

'There was an old woman who lived in a lamp,
She had no room to beetle her champ.
She ups with the beetle and broke the lamp,
And then she had room to beetle her champ.'

'Poundies', 'stampy' and 'cally' are all variations of champ – a dish composed of mashed, floury potatoes with a variety of ingredients added. The 'beetle' or poundy refers to the wooden implement with which the potatoes were beetled or pounded (they ate seriously large amounts of potatoes in those days). Historically the commonest recipe used onions of whatever kind was available. Today, scallions (spring or green onions) are most often used, but chives are also used in restaurants.

SERVES 4–6

Ingredients:

900 g/2 lbs floury potatoes
1 large bunch scallions (about 1 cup), chopped
250 ml/8 fl oz/1 cup milk
butter to taste

Method:

Steam the potatoes (preferably in their skins). Dry using an absorbent cloth or tea towel, then peel. Chop the scallions and simmer in the milk for a minute or two. Keep warm. Put the potatoes through a potato ricer or mouli, or mash thoroughly. Add the milk and scallion mixture, season to taste and mix thoroughly, but lightly. You may add more milk if the mixture seems dry, but on no account should it become wet.

Reheat until piping hot. This can be done most conveniently in a microwave oven at a medium setting for 5-7 minutes. Place each serving on a very hot plate, make a 'dunt' (depression) in the centre and put a good knob of butter in, allowing it to melt into a little lake. Eat from the outside in, dipping each forkful into the butter.

Variations:

Substitute 1 cup of cooked peas or broad beans (skinned and finely chopped) for the scallions; or cooked chopped onion, cooked mashed parsnip, or cooked and mashed turnip (swede), or finely chopped young nettle tops (cooked in the milk until tender), or cooked chopped spinach. Chives, parsley, or wild garlic (finely chopped) are added directly to the potato rather than cooked in the milk first.

"beetle"

celeriac and potato purée

Celeriac is a vegetable with a high water content and makes for a softer, wetter purée than traditional champ dishes. Its knobbly appearance puts off many people, but the flavour, which is similar to celery, makes it an especially good accompaniment to game.

SERVES 4–6

Ingredients:

450 g/1 lb floury potatoes, peeled

700 g/1½ lbs celeriac (weighed *after* peeling)

60 g/2 oz butter

30 ml/1 fl oz/⅛ cup cream

Method:

Steam the potatoes until tender. Dry and put through a potato ricer or mouli. Cut the celeriac into large chunks and boil in salted water until tender. Drain, then dry off in the pan. Purée in a food processor. Combine the two vegetables then add butter and cream, season to taste and mix well. Serve very hot.

Celeriac

'How is it that your country has so many and so healthy children?'
'Tis the praties, sir.'
18th-century Irish peasant's reply to a French traveller.

POTATO AND CHESTNUT PURÉE

Good with goose, duck and game birds like pheasant and wild duck. Chestnuts (being very troublesome to prepare) are usually bought ready-cooked and peeled. Excellent French, or Italian cooked, peeled, whole chestnuts (marrons or marroni) can be bought shrink-wrapped in good speciality shops. Tinned cooked ones are available in most supermarkets. Dried chestnuts are not as succulent; they can be reconstituted by soaking overnight and boiling for 30 minutes. The sweet chestnut is completely unrelated to the inedible horse chestnut, Aesculus hippocastum, which grows plentifully in Ireland and provides the conkers that little boys are so fond of.

SERVES 4

Ingredients:

450 g/1 lb floury potatoes, peeled

400 g/14 oz/2 cups whole, cooked chestnuts (weighed when cooked and peeled)

90 g/3 oz butter

60 ml/2 fl oz/¼ cup cream

Method:

Steam the potatoes until tender; dry, then put through a potato ricer or mouli. Purée the cooked chestnuts with the cream in a food processor. Mix with the potatoes and butter. Season to taste and serve very hot.

Chestnuts

CHAPTER ONE CHAMP

This is a 'luxury champ' by Ross Lewis, head chef at Chapter One *restaurant in* Dublin.

SERVES 4

Ingredients:

4 large organic Rooster potatoes (these are a floury potato)

250 ml/8 fl oz/1 cup cream

110 g/4 oz /1 stick butter

4 scallions, chopped

Maldon sea salt and freshly ground black pepper

Method:

Steam or boil the potatoes in their skins. Peel them and pass through a sieve or potato ricer. Reduce* the cream and butter by half in a pot. Stir in the scallions. Dry off the potatoes in a heavy pan and then add the cream and butter mixture. Season with crushed Maldon sea salt and freshly ground black pepper.

*Melt butter. Add the cream. Simmer, stirring, until the sauce thickens and its volume is reduced by half.

happy heart potato mashes

A while ago I was asked to develop recipes that pandered to the Irish fondness for flavoured mashed potato but which contained little fat – part of the effort to keep Irish hearts happy and healthy. From this came Apple Mash and Leek Mash, both of which I like so I don't feel at all deprived when I eat them.

apple mash

SERVES 6

Ingredients:

900 g/2 lbs floury potatoes, peeled

450 g/1 lb cooking apples, cored and peeled (Bramleys or similar fluffy apple)

1 teasp chopped fresh sage (optional)

Method:

Steam the potatoes until tender, then put them through a potato ricer or mouli, or mash until not a single lump remains. Slice the apples and cook until soft in just 2 tablespoons of water. Beat with a wooden spoon until completely smooth. Mix into the potato with the sage, salt and freshly ground white (or black) pepper. Serve hot.

Leek mash

SERVES 6

Ingredients:

900 g/2 lbs floury potatoes, peeled

450 g/1 lb leeks, cleaned and trimmed

2-3 tablesp parsley, chopped

salt and freshly ground black pepper

Method:

Steam the potatoes until tender, drain, then put through a potato ricer or mouli, or mash until not a single lump remains. Slice the cleaned leek into thin diagonal strips. Place in a little boiling water and simmer for about 5 minutes, or until tender. Drain. Use a wooden spoon to mix the leek, the parsley, salt and freshly ground pepper into the potatoes. Serve hot.

ROSEMARY AND CASHEL BLUE CHEESE MASH

Derry Clarke, chef/patron of Dublin's renowned l'Ecrivain restaurant, is noted for putting a contemporary spin on traditional Irish dishes. His recipe uses one of Ireland's most famous farmhouse cheeses, Cashel Blue, which is made in Fethard, County Tipperary, near the famous Rock of Cashel.

SERVES 4

Ingredients:

4 large Rooster potatoes

4 small sprigs of fresh rosemary

4 shallots, peeled and finely chopped

2 cloves of garlic, peeled, crushed and finely chopped

250 ml/8 fl oz/1 cup cream

4 tablesp butter

110 g/4 oz/8 level tablesp Cashel Blue cheese

Method:

Steam or boil the potatoes in their skins. Peel and dry them and pass through a mouli or potato ricer. Melt half the butter in a pan over a medium heat. Add the shallots and garlic and sweat gently for 1 minute without browning. Add the remaining butter, cream and the rosemary. Cook until reduced by half. Strain. Off the heat add the cheese and set aside for 2 minutes to allow the cheese to melt to a stringy consistency. Mix with the potatoes, season to taste and serve hot.

The Rock of Cashel

COLCANNON

For a dish that is not widely eaten today, colcannon remains remarkably widely known. And it has the distinction of having a song dedicated to it, a song that, like the recipe itself, has two versions. If you say 'colcannon' in a crowded room, chances are that half the room will break into one version of the song and the other half into a completely different version.

COLCANNON MADE WITH KALE:

'Did you ever eat colcannon when 'twas made with yellow cream
And the kale and praties blended like the picture in a dream?
Did you ever take a forkful and dip it in the lake
Of heather-flavoured butter that your mother used to make?
Oh you did, yes you did! So did he and so did I,
And the more I think about it sure, the more I want to cry.'

COLCANNON MADE WITH CABBAGE:

'Did you ever eat colcannon when 'twas made with thickened cream
And the greens and scallions blended like the picture in a dream?
Did you ever scoop a hole on top to hold the melting cake
Of clover-flavoured butter which your mother used to make?
Did you ever eat and eat, afraid you'd let the ring go past,
And some old married sprissman would get it at the last?'

BOTH VERSIONS END WITH:

'God be with the happy times when trouble we had not
And our mothers made colcannon in the little three-legged pot.'

Colcannon is so like champ, cally, stampy and poundies that it is difficult to understand how it ever came to have a different name. Yet, all over the country, colcannon is colcannon and known as nothing else. As in the two versions of the song, it can be made with kale or with greens – meaning cabbage. Those reared on the version made with kale don't accept the cabbage version as colcannon and those in the other camp, I'm sure, are equally insistent that their method is the true one. I was reared without the addition of scallions and feel they interfere with the very individual taste of kale. Others would maintain that they are an essential ingredient.

Colcannon is eaten at Hallowe'en when the kale crop is ready, and often had a ring put into it as a 'favour' – a tradition taken over by barm brack in most parts of Ireland today.

SERVES 6–8

Ingredients:

1 kg/2½ lbs floury potatoes, peeled

250 ml/8 fl oz/1 cup curly kale*, cooked and finely chopped

250 ml/8 fl oz/1 cup hot milk

1 bunch (about 6) scallions, finely chopped (optional)

4 tablesp butter

* For 'Cabbage Colcannon' omit the kale and substitute 250 ml/8 fl oz/1 cup finely chopped green cabbage

Method:

Steam the potatoes until tender. Dry off by placing a clean tea-towel on top for a few minutes. Then put through a potato ricer or mouli.

Strip the soft kale leaf away from the stem and tougher veins. Discard the stem and veins. Shred the leaves finely. Bring a large, stainless-steel pot of salted water to a furious boil, add the kale leaves and cook until just tender. Drain and cool immediately under cold running water – vital if you wish to preserve its bright green colour. Drain, then squeeze out any excess liquid. Place the kale in a food processor with the hot milk and process until you have a thick green 'soup'.

Put the scallions (if using) in a small pan with the butter and soften for just 30 seconds.

Lightly, but thoroughly, mix the scallions, potatoes and kale until you have a pale green fluff. Season with salt and freshly ground black pepper, then reheat until piping hot in the microwave or (covered) in an oven. Serve with more butter.

CORNED BEEF WITH COLCANNON

Colcannon is the perfect accompaniment for corned beef, for boiled ham, for sausages, and for many other meats and fishes. Corned beef has been a standard on the Irish family dinner table for generations. It is mentioned in the eleventh-century Irish dream poem, 'Aishlinge Meic ConGlinne':

> 'Many wonderful provisions
> Pieces of palatable food
> Full without fault
> Perpetual joints of corned beef'

Traditional sauces to accompany corned (or spiced) beef and colcannon are a simple white parsley sauce or a mustard sauce.

SERVES 6

Ingredients:

1.5 kg/about 3 lbs corned beef

1 onion

1 carrot

bouquet garni

2 cloves garlic

500 ml/1 pt/2 cups/(small bottle) dry cider

Method:

Soak the meat (overnight if possible), changing the water several times to remove some of the salt used in the curing process. Put all the ingredients in a large oven-proof pot with water to cover. Bring to the boil, skimming all the while. Reduce heat to a bare simmer and cover tightly. Cooked in the oven at 150°C/300°F/Gas 2 it takes between 45 and 60 minutes per ½ kg/1 lb. Tenderness varies, so test when three-quarters of the cooking time has elapsed. Serve with colcannon.

If you intend to eat the meat cold, allow it to cool in its cooking water, remove and press it lightly by placing in a dish just large enough to fit the joint. Cover with a plate weighed down with, eg, a couple of 450g tins of tomatoes.

INDIAN 'DRY' POTATOES WITH ONIONS

This is a simple potato dish of Madhur Jaffrey's that has become a firm favourite in our house. It can be served either as a dish on its own (eaten with Indian breads like chapatis, pooris, or parathas), or as an accompaniment to a roast.

SERVES 4

Ingredients:

6 medium-sized potatoes (floury or yellow-fleshed potatoes work equally well)

5 tablesp vegetable oil

$\frac{1}{8}$ teasp ground asafoetida

$\frac{1}{2}$ teasp whole cumin seeds

$2\frac{1}{2}$ teasp whole black mustard seeds

1-3 whole dried red chilli peppers (one pepper will make it mildly 'hot')

1 medium-sized onion, peeled and coarsely chopped

$\frac{1}{2}$ teasp ground turmeric

$1\frac{1}{4}$ teasp salt

1 teasp garam masala powder

2 tablesp lemon juice

Method:

Boil the potatoes in their jackets. Peel them and mash them coarsely with a fork or hand-masher. Heat the oil in a 25-30 cm/10-12 inch frying-pan over medium heat. When hot, first put in the asafoetida; when it has sizzled for only a few seconds, add the cumin and mustard seeds; then in 10 seconds or so, the red chilli pepper (or peppers). When the pepper changes colour (1-5 seconds), put in the chopped onions and turmeric. After the onions have cooked for 3-5 minutes and turned brown at the edges, put in the mashed potatoes, salt, garam masala and lemon juice. Fry, stirring and mixing, for 5-7 minutes. Place in a warmed dish and serve.

BOXTY ON THE GRIDDLE

'Boxty on the griddle,
    Boxty in the pan
    If you don't eat your boxty
    You'll never get a man.'
And the answering rhyme chanted by the young women is instructive:
    'I'll have none of your boxty
    I'll have none of your blarney
    But I'll throw my petticoats over my head
    And be off with my royal Charlie.'

Boxty is perhaps the most individual of our traditional potato dishes. It differs from other European dishes using grated raw potato in that cooked mashed potato and flour are also added. It is particularly associated with the northern midlands and the province of Ulster. Boxty must be cooked as soon as it is prepared lest the raw potatoes turn black.

SERVES 4–6

Ingredients:

450 g/1 lb raw floury
potatoes, peeled

450 g/1 lb cooked floury
potatoes, mashed while
warm

110 g/4 oz/1 cup plain white
flour

salt

Method:

Grate the raw potatoes directly into a clean cloth. Holding the cloth over a bowl, twist the ends of the cloth together tightly and wring out all the starchy liquid from the potatoes into the bowl. The wrung potatoes are placed in another bowl and covered with the mashed potatoes (this prevents the grated potatoes becoming discoloured). The liquid in the first bowl settles and the starch drops to the bottom. Carefully pour off the clear liquid at the top. Then mix the starch thoroughly with the grated and mashed potatoes. Sift the flour with a good pinch of salt mixed in, then knead into the potato mix as if you were kneading bread dough. Roll out on a floured board and cut into farls (triangles), squares or circles about 1.5 cm/½ inch thick. (Makes 4-8 depending on shape.)

Heat a heavy griddle (or frying-pan), which has been very lightly greased. Cook the boxty cakes slowly until well browned on both sides. They are best eaten hot, fresh from the pan, lightly buttered.

Traditionally boxty cakes were fried in bacon fat for breakfast. If this is your plan you might make them thicker and then slice each cake in two horizontally before frying.

the Full Irish, with Boxty

BOXTY IN THE PAN

A good deal more flour is used in this recipe, and also buttermilk together with bicarbonate of soda. The resulting mixture makes boxty potato pancakes.

SERVES 6

Ingredients:

225 g/9 oz raw floury potatoes, peeled

255 g/9 oz floury potatoes, cooked and mashed while warm

255 g/9 oz/2¼ cups plain white flour, **or** finely ground wholewheat flour

½ teasp bicarbonate of soda

300-400 ml/10-14 fl oz/ (generous) 1¼-1½ cups of buttermilk

Method:

Grate the potatoes and extract the starch in exactly the same way as for boxty on the griddle. Sift the flour and bicarbonate of soda and mix thoroughly with the grated and mashed potato mixture. Add enough buttermilk to make a thick pancake batter. Season with salt and freshly ground black pepper. Cook immediately to prevent the raw potato turning black as a result of oxidisation. Drop spoonfuls – just enough to form small cakes about 8 cm/3 inches across – onto a heated, lightly greased pan and cook until well-browned on each side and cooked through.

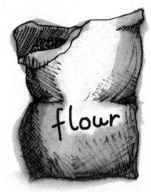

OVEN-BAKED BOXTY

The addition of fat and baking powder produces something nearer to a scone.

MAKES 8

Ingredients:

255 g/9 oz floury potatoes, grated raw

255 g/9 oz floury potatoes, cooked and mashed

255 g/9 oz/2¼ cups plain white flour

½ teasp baking powder

2 tablesp melted bacon fat, **or** butter

a little buttermilk, **or** fresh milk

Method:

Sift the flour, baking powder and a good pinch of salt together and make exactly as you would griddle boxty except that the butter or bacon fat is added before stirring in sufficient milk or buttermilk to make a firm dough.

Divide into 2 pieces, roll out on a floured board, then divide into farls or cut into circles with a scone-cutter. Bake at 180°C/350°F/Gas 4 for 30-40 minutes.

Eat hot from the oven, split and buttered.

BOXTY DUMPLINGS

These can be used instead of dumplings made from flour and are a good accompaniment to stews, casseroles and to boiled bacon, or corned beef and spiced beef.

MAKES 16

Ingredients:

255 g/9 oz floury potatoes, raw and grated

255 g/9 oz floury potatoes, cooked and mashed

110 g/4 oz/1 cup plain white flour (approx.)

1 teasp salt

Method:

Prepare in the same way as boxty on the griddle. The amount of flour varies depending on the flouriness of the potatoes – use enough to make a pliable dough. After kneading, form into balls about the size of a golf ball. Drop into boiling salted water and simmer for 40-45 minutes.

Old Ways: In country areas, cooked potatoes were tipped into a flat osier basket – a skib – from which the cooking moisture could escape. In grander households they used a delicately worked silver potato ring in which a linen napkin was placed to absorb the moisture.

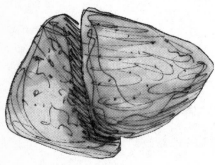

LITTLE POTATO PANCAKES

A cross between a pancake and a potato cake, these tasty morsels are good on their own, or as a vegetable side dish, or to accompany The Full Irish Breakfast.

MAKES 20

Ingredients:

4 large floury potatoes, cooked and mashed while hot

2 eggs

3 tablesp plain white flour

1 teasp baking powder

200 ml/7 fl oz/¾ cup of milk

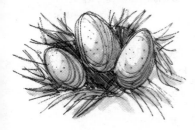

Method:

Whisk together the eggs, flour, baking powder and about half the milk. Quickly stir in the mashed potatoes and mix really well. Add enough milk to make a thick batter. Season with salt and freshly ground black pepper.

Choose a wide non-stick pan or griddle; heat it and grease lightly. Drop as many tablespoonfuls of the batter as you can fit onto the hot griddle. Cook for about 3 minutes or until bubbles rise to the surface and the underside is well browned. Turn over with a palette knife and brown the other side. Keep hot while you cook the rest of the batter.

Variations:

Add chopped scallions, crisply cooked and finely chopped bacon rashers, or cooked and finely chopped mushrooms.

CLONAKILTY BLACK PUDDING WITH HERBED POTATO PANCAKES AND MUSTARD

This recipe comes from Chris Daly, head chef at Tinakilly House, Rathnew, County Wicklow.

SERVES 4

Ingredients:

12 slices of Clonakilty black pudding, cut 1 cm/½ inch thick

For the Potato Pancakes:

150 g/5 oz floury potatoes, cooked and mashed while hot

90 g/3 oz/¼ cup plain white flour

1 large egg

2 tablesp fresh herbs, chopped

3-4 tablesp milk

a little grated nutmeg

15 g/½ oz/1 level tablesp butter

a little oil

Method:

Grill the black pudding until just beginning to crisp. Keep warm.

In a food processor mix the potatoes, flour, egg, herbs and enough milk to loosen the consistency and make a thick batter. Season with salt, black pepper and freshly grated nutmeg. Heat a heavy pan and when hot add the butter and a little oil. Using a dessertspoon measure out 12 small pancakes. Cook on each side until golden brown and cooked through.

Place 3 pancakes on each plate with the black pudding on top, garnished with fresh parsley and with some wholegrain Irish mustard – whiskey-flavoured mustard is specially good with this dish. You may, if you wish, loosen the mustard with a little cream.

POTATO CAKES

A potato cake is a savoury, not a sweet cake. The texture of the cake varies from region to region and is achieved by using more or less flour. Commercial potato cakes are of the firm, well-floured variety to make them easy to handle and to ensure a longer shelf-life. More potato and less flour makes a moister cake that is more tender to the tooth. Thickness varies from 0.5-1 cm/¼-½ inch; cakes high in potato being thicker than those high in flour. Just to complicate the arcane craft of potato cake-making even more, you should know that in the northeast of Ireland they are usually called 'fadge', or 'tatie squares' (even when cut into triangular farls!). Whatever about the relative merits of the shape, this is a recipe worth experimenting with to find the one most to your taste. One way or the other, these are an essential part of an Ulster Fry, although not, strangely enough, of a Full Irish Breakfast.

MAKES 8–12

Ingredients:

450 g/1 lb floury potatoes, cooked and mashed hot

60-175 g/2-6 oz/½-1½ cups plain white flour

½ teasp salt

2 tablesp butter, melted

60 ml/2 fl oz/¼ cup milk (approx.)

Method:

Keep back a couple of tablespoons of the flour. Mix all the other ingredients together, adding just enough milk to make a fairly firm dough. Sprinkle the flour on a flat surface and roll the dough out to 0.5-1 cm/¼-½ inch thick. Cut into square, triangular or round shapes, as you wish. Bake on an ungreased griddle (or heavy frying-pan) until lightly brown on both sides. Serve hot from the pan, or reheat by frying in a little bacon fat or butter, or spread with very little butter and grill until warmed through.

Makes 8-12 depending on the thickness and shape chosen.

POTATO AND OAT CAKES

These substantial potato cakes have different names in different parts of Ireland: potato and oat cakes in the South, oaten potato cakes in Ulster, except in County Antrim, where, according to the food writer Florence Irwin ('the Cookin' Woman'), they are always called Rozel. She notes wryly that they are 'not suitable for invalids'.

MAKES 8

Ingredients:

350 g/12 oz floury potatoes, cooked and mashed hot

110 g/4 oz/(generous) 1 cup pinhead oatmeal

15 g/½ oz/2 tablesp butter

a good pinch of salt

Method:

Mix everything together, using a drop of milk if it seems necessary, until you have a firm dough. Roll out, shape and cook in the same manner as for Potato Cakes in the previous recipe (p.53).

POTATO PASTRY

An excellent shortcrust pastry can be made by substituting cooked potatoes for some of the flour. As with all pastries the recipes vary. The first recipe below is very rich and fat-heavy, but produces a light crust suitable for fruit or savoury pies or as a base for small tarts; the second uses only half the butter but is enriched with an egg — less delicate, but easier to handle and roll out.

Ingredients:

90 g/3 oz/¼ cup self-raising flour

90 g/3 oz floury potatoes, cooked and hot

175 g/6 oz/1½ sticks butter, very cold

pinch salt

water (only if needed)

Variation:

110 g/4 oz floury potatoes, cooked and hot

110 g/4 oz/1 cup plain white flour

½ teasp baking powder

pinch salt

90 g/3 oz/¾ stick butter

1 small egg, beaten

Method 1:

Put the hot potatoes through a potato ricer or mouli and allow to cool. Sift the flour and salt. Rub the butter into the flour and then, as lightly as possible, mix in the potato. Add water if necessary. Knead lightly and roll out as you would for shortcrust pastry.

Method 2:

Put the hot potatoes through a potato ricer or mouli and allow to cool. Sift flour, salt and baking powder together. Rub in the butter, stir in the potatoes lightly and just enough beaten egg to make a firm dough. Roll out on a floured board and use for both sweet and savoury dishes.

Makes enough pastry for a 20 cm/8 inch flan tin.

Old Ways: In autumn the Gaelic Irish buried tubs of butter to last them the winter. Finds of long-forgotten caches — bog butter — are said to be still edible.

RHUBARB TART

The rhubarb patch survives in gardens all over Ireland and it remains a favourite filling for tarts as well as being used extensively in jams and preserves. This is a classic Irish tart-filling during spring and early summer.

SERVES 4–6

Ingredients:

900 g/2 lbs rhubarb

110 g/4 oz/1 cup sugar

1 egg white, beaten until stiff

potato pastry (Double the quantity of either of the two potato pastry recipes on p.55)

Method:

Clean and cut up the rhubarb into short lengths. Place in a pan with the sugar and simmer for about 10 minutes or until the rhubarb is barely tender. Then fold in the egg white thoroughly and cool. Line a 25 cm/ 10 inch tart tin with half the pastry. Pour in the rhubarb and top with the remaining pastry. Seal the edges with a fork. Bake at 200°C/400°F/Gas 6 for about 35 minutes, or until the pastry is cooked through and golden brown.

apple fadge

In County Antrim the many small bakeries that were once famous in Ulster used to make fadge. The origins of the word are unknown – it is neither Gaelic nor, apparently, Ulster-Scots. It is used variously to denote a thick wheaten loaf, a potato cake baked on the griddle, or a large piece of oatcake, or indeed an irregular piece of almost anything. Here, and in the small bakeries where it was once made, it means a savoury potato cake stuffed with apples. It is good eaten hot with grilled sausages, or with roast pork, duck or goose.

MAKES 4

Ingredients:

450 g/1 lb floury potatoes, cooked, mashed hot

a good pinch of salt

2 tablesp butter

110 g/4 oz/1 cup plain white flour

250 ml/8 fl oz/1 cup cooked, fluffy apple purée

Method:

Mix the potatoes, flour, butter and salt together and knead lightly. Divide into 4 and roll out into four circles. Divide the apple purée evenly between them, placing it on one side of the circle only. Fold the other side over, as if you were making a turnover, or pasty. Seal the edges well by pinching together firmly, so they do not open while cooking. Place on a baking tray and bake at 200°C/400°F/Gas 6 for about 20 minutes, or until brown and crisp. Serve hot.

Cook's Tip:

Although Bramley apples make the fluffiest purée, it is quite a sour apple, which you may like to sweeten with a little sugar.

potato apple farls

A farl is a triangular shape – the traditional shape for potato cakes and griddle bread as well as for these rather unusual apple pastries. In some parts of the country these were served at Hallowe'en with the ring or favour placed in just one cake. Originally they would have been cooked on a griddle over an open turf fire. They can be cooked on a heavy frying-pan, or baked in a hot oven.

MAKES 4

Ingredients:

480 g/1 lb floury potatoes, mashed while hot

480 g/1 lb/4 cups white flour

15 g/½ oz/1 tablesp butter, melted

½ teasp baking powder

4 large cooking apples (Bramley, if possible), peeled, cored and thinly sliced

honey, or brown sugar and butter, to taste

Method:

Sift the flour and baking powder, mix in a bowl with the melted butter and the hot, mashed potatoes. Mix well and knead lightly until you have a soft dough. Divide into 2 equal pieces.

On a floured board roll out 1 piece of the dough into a circle 1.5 cm/½ inch thick. Divide into 4 farls (triangles). Repeat with the second piece of dough. On all 4 of the farls place an equal amount of apple. Place another farl on top of each one and pinch the edges together to seal well.

Cook over a medium heat on a griddle or in a heavy frying-pan until brown on the bottom. Turn carefully and brown the other side. Now comes the tricky bit! Slit the pastries lengthways and lift off the tops. Add thin slices of butter and (depending how sweet you like a dessert to be) as much honey or sugar as you fancy. Carefully replace the tops and continue cooking in the pan for a few minutes until the butter and sugar have melted into a sauce. Serve hot.

BASIC POTATO SOUP

Floury potatoes are used as a base and a thickening agent in a wide range of Irish soups as well as for this classic plain potato soup (which, of course, uses other, stronger vegetables to flavour the potatoes — leeks, onions, or celery). It's especially good made on a stock from chicken or turkey carcass. It can be served as a vegetable broth or puréed. Any number of garnishes may be used to enhance it: croutons — garlic-flavoured, or plain; crisp cubes of chopped bacon; small cubes of crisp fried potatoes; a few peppery watercress leaves; some chopped dill or chives; or a swirl of whipped cream.

SERVES 6

Ingredients:

1 kg/2¼ lbs floury potatoes, peeled (and quartered if large)

2 medium onions, peeled and chopped, **or** 2 large leeks cleaned and sliced finely

1 stick celery, finely chopped (optional)

2 tablesp butter

1½ ltrs/2⅓ pts/about 6 cups half milk/half water, **or** poultry stock

3-4 tablesp chopped parsley, or chives

a little lightly whipped cream (optional)

Method:

Melt the butter in a heavy pan and sweat the onions or leeks (together with the celery if using) over a gentle heat until soft but not brown. Add the liquid and the potatoes, season with salt and freshly ground black pepper, then simmer until the potatoes are tender. Purée in a food mill or food processor, return to the pan and reheat. Check seasoning and serve hot garnished with herbs and a little cream.

Variations:

To this basic recipe you can add chopped, crisply cooked bacon, or a little leftover cooked ham, or even diced cooked sausage. Give it a seafood treatment by adding chopped cooked prawns, scallops, mussels, or clams.

Ring the changes with different fresh herbs: dill, mint, marjoram, or even a little rosemary.

POTATO AND NETTLE SOUP

Nettles are an ancient spring tonic reputed to clear all toxins from the system. Young nettle tops picked in spring and early summer are best. You can treat your nettles as a cut-and-come-again vegetable – if you keep harvesting the tops for kitchen use before they flower you'll be rewarded by a supply of tender tops until autumn. They do not sting once cooked – but you'd be advised to firmly 'grasp the nettle' (more fool you) or wear gloves when picking them!

SERVES 6

Ingredients:

350 g/12 oz/2 cups floury potatoes, peeled and diced (1 cm/½ inch)

150 g/5 oz/1 cup onions, peeled and chopped

300 g/10 oz/2 cups (well-packed) nettle tops

1.25 ltrs/2 pts/5 cups chicken or turkey stock

30 g/1 oz/2 tablesp butter (or bacon, or goose fat)

Garnish:

chopped chives and a little whipped cream

Method:

Heat the butter in the pot and sweat the onion gently until soft. Add the stock and the potatoes, bring to the boil and simmer for 10-15 minutes until the potatoes are tender. Add nettle tops and simmer for 5 minutes.
Purée in a blender or food processor or pass through a mouli.
Season to taste and reheat before serving. Garnish with chopped chives and a swirl of cream.

Nettles

pOTaTO aNÒ LeeK sOUP

Leeks have been eaten in Ireland since ancient times and the combination of leeks and spuds was popular in Ireland long before the classic American (or French) chilled Vichyssoise. Needless to say, in Ireland we eat this soup hot.

SERVES 6

Ingredients:

4 large leeks

4 large floury potatoes, peeled and chopped

1 ltr/1 1/3 pts/4 cups hot chicken stock

4 tablesp butter

Garnish:

chopped chives, or parsley, and a little lightly whipped cream

Method:

It is in the nature of leeks to trap earth as they grow, so they must be thoroughly cleaned. Start by removing the root end and any wilted or discoloured outer leaves. Leave as much of the green part intact as you can. Make a crossways cut down through the green part. Invert the cut ends in a large jug of cold water and whoosh each leek up and down a few times. Leave them inverted in the water for several hours. In theory, all the earth will drop out into the water; in practice, you may still need to clean the last grains out by placing the green ends under running water. Slice into rings.

Melt the butter in a heavy-based pan, add the leeks, cover and cook gently for about 10 minutes. Add the potatoes and stir well to coat them in the butter. Add the hot stock. Cover and simmer for about 10 more minutes, or until the potatoes are tender. Purée in a food processor or mouli and season to taste with salt and black pepper.

Serve hot, garnished with chopped chives and a swirl of cream.

seafood chowder with dillisk and carrageen

The Irish are very fond of seafood chowder and you will find it on the menu of bars and restaurants the length and breadth of the country. This recipe is by Colm Wyse of the Dublin Institute of Technology (the institution where a great number of Ireland's youngest and finest chefs begin their training). It featured on BIM's (the Irish Sea Fisheries Board) calendar of seafood dishes by students training to be chefs. Dillisk and Carrageen are the two most commonly eaten seaweeds used in traditional Irish cooking. Not only do they add flavour but act as a natural thickening agent.

SERVES 6–8

Ingredients:

450 g/1 lb pollock, cod, or other white fish fillets

225 g/8 oz shellfish (mussels, cockles, prawns)

110 g/4 oz salmon, cubed

25 g/1 oz/¼ stick butter

60 g/2 oz streaky bacon, cut into matchstick strips

1 kg/2 lbs mixed vegetables (onions, leeks, carrots, celery, waxy potatoes), diced

570 ml/1 pt/2¼ cups water

7 g/¼ oz dillisk *

7 g/¼ oz Carrageen **

570 ml/1 pt/2¼ cups milk

Garnish:

fresh parsley and chives

* Dillisk is a purple-reddish seaweed found off the Irish coast. It has the highest iron content of any known edible food source and is very rich in protein.

** Carrageen (also known as Irish moss) is a bushy, reddish-purple seaweed found abundantly around the Irish coast. It is rich in calcium and other essential vitamins and minerals.

Method:

Cook the bacon strips in butter until crisp. Add all the vegetables except the potatoes. Season with a little salt and freshly ground black pepper and cook slowly without colouring for 5 minutes. Add water, dillisk and Carrageen and cook for 10 minutes. Add the potatoes and milk and cook until potatoes are soft. Add fish and shellfish and cook for 3-5 minutes.

Check seasoning and serve sprinkled with chopped parsley and chives.

fish anд potato cakes

These can be made with pretty well any fish, but a particular favourite in Ireland is pollock. There's a good reason for this. It is a fish commonly caught while fishing off rocks around the coast of Ireland. Rock fishermen and women may set out to fish for mackerel, ling, wrasse or bass, but invariably come back with 'half a tonne' of pollock. It's not a particularly well-regarded fish to eat neat, but improves in flavour when gutted the moment it's caught and then kept for twenty-four hours — when it makes grand fish cakes! Because they're a little troublesome to make, you might as well make several dozen at a time. This works out fine because fish cakes freeze well. This recipe makes four. Just scale it up depending on your catch.

Ingredients:

350 g/12 oz cooked fish, skinned, boned and flaked

350 g/12 oz floury potatoes, cooked and mashed

2 teasp capers, rinsed, drained and chopped,

or 2 teasp scallions, finely chopped

2 tablesp fresh parsley, chives, or dill, finely chopped

1 tablesp fresh lemon juice (optional)

For the coating:

2 small eggs, beaten

2 tablesp plain white flour

about 6 tablesp fine white breadcrumbs

Method:

Mix all the fish cake ingredients together and season well with salt and freshly ground black pepper. Form into flat patties, rather like large hamburgers. Dip (in turn) into the flour, egg and breadcrumbs. Place in the fridge to set for at least an hour. Shallow-fry in olive oil, vegetable oil, or (preferably) bacon fat until brown and crisp on both sides.

Cook's Tip:

These cakes are good served with grilled tomatoes, mushrooms and hot toast for breakfast.

For lunch serve with a spicy salsa or a Thai dipping sauce. Another good accompaniment is Wild Garlic and Cream sauce (recipe p.65).

WILD GARLIC AND CREAM SAUCE

Perfect served with the Fish and Potato Cakes (opposite), this creamy, flavour-filled sauce is also good with grilled or baked fish, with shellfish and with plainly cooked vegetables. It uses wild garlic, which can be found growing in profusion in the hedgerows of Ireland. Wild garlic has a white flowerhead on a green stem and long, thin leaves. Unlike its domesticated relative, it is the leaves, and not the bulb, which are used in cooking. It has a more subtle flavour than regular garlic.

Ingredients:

60 g/2 oz wild garlic leaves
110 g/4 oz/1 stick butter
4 tablesp cream
2-3 tablesp dry white wine
a little fresh lemon juice

Method:

Wash, dry, then chop the garlic leaves and whiz in a food processor with the butter. Chill. In a small pot bring the cream and wine to the boil and reduce by half. Turn heat to very low and whisk in the wild garlic butter mixture a little at a time. Season to taste with lemon juice.

This sauce is best served at once. It does not reheat well but can be kept barely warm.

'Sauce of the poor man – a little
potato with a big one.'
An Irish saying.

woodcock smokery kippers with potato salad and poached egg

Kippers are herrings that have been hot-smoked. They have been eaten in Ireland since ancient times. This recipe is by Ross Lewis of Chapter One restaurant in Dublin. It was prepared for the luncheon at which the Irish Food Writers Guild announced their Food Award winners for 2001. Sally Barnes's Woodcock Smokery kippers won a major award and are spectacularly good.

SERVES 4

Ingredients:

6 baby waxy potatoes (like Nicola or Charlotte)

a little white wine vinegar

4 small eggs

4 Woodcock Smokery kippers

15 g/½ oz/1 level tablesp unsalted butter

a little olive oil

1 tablesp snipped fresh chives

4 fresh chervil sprigs

For the mustard beurre blanc:

125 ml/4 fl oz/½ cup tarragon vinegar

60 ml/2 fl oz/¼ cup dry white wine

2 shallots, very finely chopped

60 ml/2 fl oz/¼ cup double cream

135 g/4½ oz/(generous) 1 stick unsalted butter, chilled and diced

1 tablesp wholegrain mustard

½ tablesp Dijon mustard

Maldon sea salt and freshly ground black pepper

Method:

Place the potatoes in a pan of boiling salted water, cover, then bring back to the boil. Reduce the heat and simmer for 15-20 minutes until tender. Drain and leave to cool a little, then carefully peel away the skins and cut each potato into 2 even-sized rounds, discarding the rounded ends.

Heat a large, deep pan two-thirds full with water, and add 1 tablespoon of vinegar for each 1.2 litres/2 pints of water. Bring to the boil, then break the eggs one at a time into where the water is bubbling. Reduce the heat and simmer gently for 3 minutes, then carefully remove the eggs with a slotted spoon into a large bowl of iced water to prevent further cooking. When cold, trim any ragged ends from the cooked egg whites.

To make the mustard *beurre blanc*, place the vinegar, wine and shallots in a small pan and reduce to 2 tablespoons. Stir in the cream. Reduce the heat to very low, whisk in the butter cubes a few at a time, adding the next batch just before the butter already in the pan is entirely melted. Whisk all the time. Stir in both mustards and season to taste. Keep warm over a very, very low heat.

Heat the oven to 220°C/450°F/Gas 7, or the grill to high. Arrange the kippers on a baking sheet and dot with the butter. Place in the oven or under the grill for 2-3 minutes until warm (not hot). Remove the skin and keep warm. Heat the olive oil in a sauté pan, add the potato rounds, season and just warm through, tossing occasionally. Place the poached eggs in a pan of gently simmering, salted water for 1 minute to heat through.

To serve, arrange 3 pieces of potato on each plate and add the kippers. Place the poached eggs on top and cover with the mustard *beurre blanc*. Season to taste and sprinkle over the chopped chives, then garnish with the chervil sprigs.

'Our gentry who fed on turtle and wine,
Must now eat wet lumpers and on salt herrings dine.'
Anon.

POTATO AND FISH STEW

An adaptable dish that works well with most fish. It certainly does something for less interesting fish, like whiting, pollock and farmed trout or salmon.

SERVES 4

Ingredients:

8 yellow-fleshed potatoes, peeled and sliced

2 onions, peeled and sliced

4 large carrots, scrubbed and chopped

4 stalks celery, chopped

2 tablesp olive oil

juice of 1 large lemon

4 fillets or cutlets of fish

1 large bunch fresh parsley, finely chopped

500 ml/16 fl oz/2 cups water, or fish stock

Method:

Put water or stock in a large, wide pot or a deep frying-pan with a lid. Add 1 tablespoon of oil. Add the vegetables and bring to simmering point. Cook gently for about 15 minutes or until the vegetables are nearly tender. Meanwhile, skin the fish and cut into bite-sized pieces. Place fish pieces on top of the vegetables, add the rest of the oil and the lemon juice and season to taste. Cover and steam until the fish is just opaque and flakes reasonably easily – how long this takes depends on the variety of fish and how thick the pieces are. Don't overcook and serve as soon as it is ready. Ladle onto hot soup plates, sprinkle generously with parsley and a little more lemon juice if you wish. Eat with a fork and spoon.

slow-cooked potato and vegetable omelette

Spain has the tortilla, Italy its frittata and the Middle East its eggah – none of them terribly different, just regional 'spin' applied to a slow-cooked omelette with more filling than egg.

SERVES 4

Ingredients:

5 large eggs

2 large waxy potatoes, peeled

1 large onion, peeled and sliced

about 2 tablesp olive oil, or butter and oil mixed

For the filling:

Make your own choice from:

a few cherry tomatoes, halved

a couple of crisply grilled rashers of bacon

the flesh of a sweet pepper, or a similar quantity of cooked vegetables, like courgette, aubergine, cauliflower, broccoli, or celeriac. Don't be tempted to use the likes of cabbage, carrots, or turnip – they just don't work.

You can even add things like leftover sausages, cooked fish, or cooked ham (but not lamb, pork, or beef). The main thing is not to cram too many flavours together all at once.

Method:

Heat the oil (or the oil and butter) in a large, deep, non-stick frying-pan. Add the sliced potatoes and other uncooked vegetables and cook gently until tender but not too soft. Lift from the pan.

Wipe out the pan with kitchen paper and heat another tablespoon of oil over a medium heat. Mix together the eggs, all the vegetables (plus whatever other additions have taken your fancy) and season with salt and black pepper. Pour into the pan and reduce the heat at once to very low. Cook until the bottom is brown and firm. Loosen the bottom from the pan with a spatula, then invert on to a suitably sized plate. Slide it back into the pan to cook the other side (just as gently) until cooked through but not dry.

Serve hot, or at room temperature, cut into wedges.

Ubh gan salann, póg gan croimbhéal.

(An egg without salt is like a kiss from a beardless man.)

CORNED BEEF HASH

In days gone by, vast quantities of corned or salt beef (when this was the only method of preserving meat) were exported from Ireland. It was also the only beef many Irish people ever ate except on festive days, like Christmas. Indeed, boiled corned beef served with parsley sauce and cabbage vied with bacon and cabbage as the nation's favourite meat dish. Corned beef hash* makes good use of the leftovers and is still a great favourite with children of all ages.

SERVES 4

Ingredients:

450 g/1 lb cooked corned or spiced beef, cut into cubes

900 g/2 lbs floury potatoes, freshly cooked, cut into large cubes

225 g/8 oz onions, peeled and chopped

4 tablesp parsley, or leftover parsley sauce

60 g/2 oz/½ stick butter

Method:

Melt the butter in a large pan over a medium heat. Add the onions and cook, stirring occasionally, until just beginning to brown. Add the potatoes, corned beef, parsley and freshly ground black pepper; mix well and press down in an even layer. Cook until brown and crispy underneath. Invert over a large plate, slide back onto the pan and cook on the other side until brown and crisp. Serve cut into wedges with freshly cooked vegetables.

Variation:

Bubble and Squeak is an English version of hashed potatoes, made with unsalted beef and leftover cabbage.

*Hash comes from the French word *bacher*, meaning 'to chop', and only came into the English language in the seventeenth century. 'You're making a total hash of it,' is a well-known Irish phrase hurled at kack-handed people who lack manual dexterity.

ÞUBLIN CODDLE

A dish rarely eaten outside Dublin. It is said to have been a favourite of Jonathan
Swift, Dean of St Patrick's Cathedral and noted author of Gulliver's Travels. In
the area of Dublin's inner city known as the Liberties, this is a Saturday night dish,
and also traditionally a funeral food – a humbler version of baked funeral meats. The
reason is purely practical – it won't spoil if left cooking for an extra hour or two!

SERVES 4–6

Ingredients:

450 g/1 lb of bacon bits*, or
a streaky bacon joint, cubed

450 g/1 lb meaty Irish
breakfast sausages

3 large onions, peeled and
chopped

1 ¼ kg/3 lbs floury and/or
waxy potatoes, peeled

6 tablesp fresh parsley,
chopped

freshly ground black pepper

500 ml/16 fl oz/2 cups water

* Bacon bits are off-cuts
from various types of bacon.
They are sold cheaply in
Dublin pork butcher shops
specifically for coddle and
contain a fairly even mixture
of fat and lean. Streaky
bacon also works well; keep
the skin on for more flavour.

Method:

Cut the potatoes into fairly large pieces
(leave whole if they are small). Choose a
heavy pot with a really tight-fitting lid. Place
a layer of chopped onions on the bottom of
the pot then layer the meat and vegetable
ingredients, giving each layer a generous
twist of freshly ground black pepper and
some chopped parsley. Bring to the boil, then
reduce the heat to a bare simmer. Cover
tightly. Cook for 2–5 hours! The longer and
slower the cooking, the better this dish will
be. Providing the lid is really tight it cannot
come to any harm. The ideal method is in a
very low oven, 120°C/250°F/Gas ½. In some
homes the look of boiled, pink sausages is
disliked. To avoid this, it is possible to set all
the sausages on the top of the coddle and just
before serving put the pot under the grill to
brown them.

Coddle is traditionally served with white
soda bread and stout. It can also be served
with quickly cooked green cabbage.

St Patrick's Cathedral, Dublin.

IRISH STEW

A simple 'white' stew that's only as good as the ingredients from which it is made. Originally made with wild kid (goat), then with mutton, and now, because we cannot easily buy either, made with lamb. Ambitious home cooks and famous chefs produce many complicated variations on this essentially simple dish – adding everything but the kitchen sink: carrots, celery, turnips, leeks, cabbage, black pudding, even cream. Some of these 'gourmet Irish stews' can be lovely to eat, but they are not, in my humble opinion, Irish stew. In its simplest form this is the comfort food of the Irish nation – put a plain, straightforward Irish stew in front of any Irishman (Unionist or Republican) and he'll devour it without fear or favour.

SERVES 4–6

Ingredients:

1.4 kg/3 lbs floury and/or waxy potatoes, peeled

900 g/2 lbs stewing lamb (gigot)

450 g/1 lb onions, chopped

5 tablesp fresh parsley, chopped

1 tablesp fresh thyme, chopped

250-500 ml/8-16 fl oz/1-2 cups of water

Method:

Peel the potatoes and leave them whole unless very large. The bones in the meat and a certain amount of fat are integral to the flavour of Irish stew; the potatoes absorb a good deal of the fat and flavour from the meat. The meat is not cubed but left in fairly large pieces. When the meat is cooked it falls away from the bone so they pose no hazard on the plate.

Place a layer of onion on the bottom of a heavy pot or casserole. Lay the meat on top. Season with salt and freshly ground black pepper and sprinkle generously with fresh parsley and rather less generously with thyme. Layer the rest of the onions with the potatoes and finish with the rest of the herbs. The amount of water required depends on how good the seal is between pot and lid. Bring to the boil and cover tightly. You may either simmer gently on the hob or cook in the oven at 150°C/300°F/Gas 2 for 2½-3 hours. The finished stew should be moist but not 'swimming' in liquid. Add a little hot water if it appears to be getting too dry for your taste. Floury potatoes will partly dissolve into the liquid (thickening it a little), waxy potatoes will not. It's a matter of taste which you use – I use some of both. Serve the stew with lots of chopped parsley. Carrots (on the side, not cooked in the stew) are a good accompaniment.

harvest festival pork and apple casserole

This is a dish that holds well – a good party dish – and is extraordinarily tasty to eat for all that the ingredients are very simple. It was (and still is) a traditional Harvest Festival dish. In Armagh, Munster and south Leinster, Michaelmas was the time to make cider and eat goose. But pork and apples are also among the foods traditionally eaten at Hallowe'en. It makes a good dish for the days after Christmas, too, as a restorative for stressed digestions. The potatoes are essential to the restorative powers, but, given the large quantities, it may be more convenient to cook them separately.

SERVES 12

Ingredients:

2.5 kg/5½ lbs floury or waxy potatoes

12 pork chops, or equivalent lean, diced pork

2 large onions, halved, then finely sliced

2 large cooking apples, peeled and sliced

2 tablesp olive oil

6-7 leaves of fresh sage, finely chopped

1 teasp ground nutmeg

450-550 ml/1 pt/(generous) 2-2¼ cups of dry cider

2 tablesp fresh parsley, finely chopped

Method:

Cut off any excess fat from the chops and remove any bones. Heat the oil and lightly fry the onions. In a wide baking dish (or dishes) large enough to hold the chops in one layer, spread out the onions. Season each layer with salt and freshly ground black pepper. If you are cooking the potatoes in the dish, slice them thickly and spread them out over the onions in an even layer. Place the chops on top and season with sage, nutmeg, salt and pepper. Spread the apple slices on top of the chops. Add the cider. Cover and bake at 160°C/325°F/Gas 3 for about 2 hours. Near the end of the cooking time, you may (if you wish) take the cover off in order to concentrate the liquid a little. Sprinkle the parsley thickly on top.

If you did not include the potatoes in the dish, serve the casserole with mashed, or plain, boiled floury potatoes.

LAMB SHANK STEW

This started out as a Turkish recipe using elderly mutton shanks. I now prefer to make it with new season baby lamb shanks (allow one shank per person) and would dearly love to find a ready source of kid (goat) shanks. Ask the butcher to saw through the bone to release the marrow.

SERVES 4–6

Ingredients:

4-6 baby lamb shanks (depending on size)

3 cloves garlic, crushed, peeled and chopped

1 teasp salt

2 teasp paprika

1x400g tin plum tomatoes

8 medium waxy potatoes, peeled

a few sprigs of fresh rosemary

Method:

Peel the garlic and pound it in a mortar with salt. When you have a creamy consistency add the paprika and stir in well. Rub the shanks all over with this mixture. Put them in a heavy pot, add the rosemary sprigs, cover with the tomatoes and their juice, then the potatoes sliced into thick (2 cm/1 inch) rings. Season well with salt and freshly ground black pepper. Bake, covered, in a moderate oven at 175°C/350°F/Gas 4 for 2 hours.

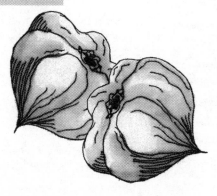

BEEF STEW

In Ireland beef stews often contain stout or ale instead of stock or water. Originally this would have been entirely dependent upon whether the brewery nearest your home made stout or beer. Like all Irish stews it is eaten with mounds of floury potatoes, but it is quite common for the potatoes to be cooked in the pot with the stew. In Dublin, certainly, the preferred cut of meat would be shin beef because when given long, slow cooking (a gentle simmering only) it softens to a melting tenderness and produces a thick, rich, gelatinous gravy.

SERVES 4

Ingredients:

450-700 g/1 lb-1½ lbs shin beef

2 large onions, peeled and chopped

2-3 carrots, peeled and sliced

8 medium waxy potatoes, peeled

30 g/1 oz/2 tablesp butter, **or** beef dripping

Small bunch of pot herbs (bay, parsley, thyme)

250 ml/8 fl oz/1 cup stout or beer

250 ml/8 fl oz/1 cup water

Method:

Melt the fat in a large frying-pan and fry the onions gently until they are translucent and beginning to brown at the edges. Remove with a slotted spoon and place with the sliced carrots in the bottom of a casserole. Remove the outer membrane from the shin beef and any large sinews. If the butcher has not done so, cut the meat into rounds about 2 cm/1 inch thick and brown them quickly in the hot fat to seal them. Remove the meat from the pan and put it in the casserole on top of the carrots, onions and the potatoes if you are cooking them in the stew. De-glaze the pan with the stout or beer. Add this liquid to the casserole along with the water, pot herbs and seasoning. Cover tightly and cook in a preheated oven at 160°C/325°F/Gas 3 for 3 hours.

Like all Irish stews, this is a flexible dish, capable of much embellishment. If you use a cut other than shin beef you may need to thicken the gravy and this should be done by dusting the meat pieces in seasoned flour before sealing them in the frying-pan. It can be further enriched by the addition of ox or lamb's kidney. It definitely improves in flavour if allowed to cool before being refrigerated and reheated after a day or two.